VOCAL SUPERSTAR:
HOW TO DEVELOP A HIGH STATUS VOICE

by Min Liu

http://www.artofverbalwar.com

Chapter 1

Introduction

*"When our words, vocal tonality, and body language all say the same thing, we become be-
lievable."*

-Paul Strikwerda

If you're reading this book, you, like me, are probably a big believer in kaizen, the Japanese word
for continuous self-improvement. You might not be familiar with that term, but I bet you're probably someone who's striving to be captivating, persuasive, and influential. Striving to become
"high status". There are many elements to becoming high status, but our VOICE is one of the
conduits by which we ultimately become high status. If you have a high status voice, you will be
seen (and heard) as more high status.

Scientists have determined that communication is not merely the words we use to communicate;
instead, communication is actually a combination of words, vocal tonality, and body language,
with each of those aspects making up roughly 10%, 30%, and 60% of communication, respec-
tively. This book is about one part of that equation, one very important part, which is vocal tonality, the 30% part.

Think about it: If you speak through a medium where people cannot see you like podcasts, radio,
or on the phone, then vocal tonality becomes the predominant factor through which you communicate. In the absence of body language as a factor, your voice and voice tonality is almost every-
thing. People cannot see you, so they cannot judge your body language, but they can hear you,
and the WAY you sound is actually much more important than WHAT you say. Yes, its obvious
we absolutely need to know what we are talking about, but the WAY we SOUND is actually 3x
more important than WHAT we say!

We are all very familiar with voices that are captivating. People like Morgan Freeman and Liam Neeson have voices that grab your attention and won't let go. You never forget them. But, even certain people in our everyday life who are not celebrities can have that same magical effect.

When was the last time somebody grabbed your attention with their voice? I'm going to give you an example of how influential someone's voice is.

I'm a corporate and securities lawyer for a Global Fortune 50 company and I'm responsible for hiring outside lawyers working at law firms to assist with important and specialized legal matters for my company when we don't have specialized lawyers on staff.

Most of these outside lawyers are competent and most of them know their stuff, and most of them present themselves pretty well. It's not hard to rationalize a decision to hire most of them, but it's also hard for them to distinguish themselves. They're all big law firm lawyers, so we know they know their stuff, they have excellent educational credentials, and they have a wealth of experience. My job is to sort through all of them and figure out who really knows their stuff and who can help us.

The truth is, I have a hard time telling one from another. It's NOT an enviable job.

I don't get to meet most of them in person, so all I have to base their competence on are usually phone calls where I quiz them about various things. I only have the content of their presentation to go on, and their voice. No matter who I talk to, their content is generally always pretty similar, as again, they all know their stuff.

However, sometimes there is that rare lawyer who has the magical ability to reach through the phone and grab you by the shoulders and shake you up with their voice and presentation. It's a very rare occurrence, but I have met (or rather...listened to) a handful of lawyers in my life whose voices projected so much authority and competence, we hired them on the spot.

Now, THAT's called having a high status voice. One that projects competence and authority so clearly its undeniable. You forget to even question what they are actually saying. That's the kind of lawyer I want representing my company in court or in important negotiations with our business partners or enemies.

Do you want to develop a speaking voice like that? I bet you do. So, let's get started!

Cheers,
Min

****

DOWNLOAD your **SPECIAL BONUS** for purchasing this book at www.artofverbalwar.com/vocalsuperstarbonus

SUBSCRIBE to my YouTube channel to learn even more about verbal and communication skills at www.youtube.com/artofverbalwar

CONTACT me at info@artofverbalwar.com

****

Chapter 2

What Does It Mean To Have A "High Status" Voice?

A high status voice has three components:

First, a high status voice sounds CERTAIN.

Second, in addition to sounding CERTAIN, a high status voice is also CAPTIVATING, i.e. it grabs your attention and doesn't let go. You WANT to hear what this captivating voice has to say.

And finally, a high status voice conveys AUTHORITY, i.e. it is dominant, authoritative, and by virtue of all three of these components, a high status voice has INFLUENCE and is MASSIVE-LY PERSUASIVE.

As you will learn later in this book, developing a high status voice is simply a matter of taking steps to:

(1) increase the **CERTAINTY** of your voice;

(2) make your voice **CAPTIVATING**; and

(3) avoid certain status lowering behaviors that relate to your voice, i.e. ensuring the **AUTHORITY** of your voice.

In the next chapter, you will learn TEN steps, each of which goes towards addressing at least one of the three elements above. By the end of this book and with deliberate practice over time, you will have a high status voice.

Chapter 3

Why Do I Want To Have A "High Status" Voice?

As I wrote earlier, research studies have determined that only about 10% of "communication" is conveyed through words. Vocal tonality makes up roughly 30-40%, and body language, the other 50-60%.

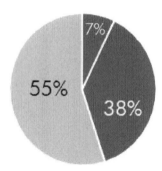

Elements of Personal Communication
- 7% spoken words
- 38% voice, tone
- 55% body language

In the book "Power Cues" by Nick Morgan, it was reported that the deeper voiced candidate in every US presidential election the past hundred years has won. He wrote: "The process of picking a leader has more to do with having the right kind of voice than it does having the right ideas or the right physique." This is definitely true, but I suspect the election results were not because of a DEEPER voice, but because of a HIGHER STATUS voice. For example, using a recent example, you may not think Obama is/was a good president, but you cannot deny that his voice is high status.

I wrote earlier: "Yes, its obvious we absolutely need to know what we are talking about, but the WAY we SOUND is actually 3x more important than WHAT we say!"

So, simply put, a high status voice and vocal tonality is a SHORTCUT to influence and persuasion. A high status voice ENSURES that what you say to others will be listened to and well received, and it also makes you much more likable, intriguing, and interesting to others.

On the flip side, a voice that does not have "high status" will be poorly received. Instead of the voice being a SHORTCUT, it becomes a SHORT CIRCUIT for influence and persuasion. The message, no matter how important, profound, or intelligent, will never be heard or received because a voice that lacks "high status" lacks certainty, authority, and the ability to grab other people's attention. Therefore, if you want to have people listen to you in the first place, be able to influence or persuade other people, or captivate them with your words, you need to develop a high status voice.

SOURCE:

"Our data imply that prosodic cues alone, when naturalistic and unambiguous, are sufficient to effectively register and interpret emotions in spoken language."

-"Emotional Speech Processing at the Intersection of Prosody and Semantics" (Schwartz R 2012)

Chapter 4

My Backstory

A while back, I had an idea that I wanted to start a podcast, so I started recording myself into my iPhone with some ideas that I had. When I listened back to the audio clips I recorded, I was shocked at how unengaging and flat I sounded.

So, I told my best friend who is also a lawyer, that I was struggling with recording myself and sounding engaging. And he said, "I probably should've told you this before, but yeah, you do have a monotone and flat voice. Sometimes it makes me want to fall asleep when I listen to you. Sorry, but its true."

That's when I realized I had to work on this aspect of my communication if I wanted to start speaking on camera or on a podcast. I started reading up, taking notes whenever I could get my hands on some information about the voice, and listening to people whose voices I admired and found dynamic, engaging, and persuasive.

And most importantly, I started practicing deliberately to improve the way my voice sounded.

Finding out the truth about ourselves is a bit painful, but it is massively important. The best way to receive some truth about ourselves is to have it done objectively and without judgment. I can't be there with you in person to tell you how you sound and how you come off, so here is an exercise for you. Record yourself speaking about something that you know about. Just do that and it will be EYE-OPENING.

No matter how you sound at the moment, I promise you that you will be able to improve your voice and increase the "status" of your voice if you implement and deliberately practice the TEN steps in this book. So, let's get on to the TEN STEPS TO A HIGH STATUS VOICE.

Chapter 5

Ten Steps to a High Status Voice

Step 1: Learn to Speak in Complete Sentences/Thoughts

This first step goes towards addressing one of the three components of a high status voice, which is CERTAINTY. I know this step almost sounds like a parent teaching a child something very basic but this concept of speaking in complete sentences/thoughts may not be anything you have actually thought about before.

It sounds so very simple, but trust me, it's not easy. This could be THE most important step in this entire book; if you take away nothing else, I hope this step is the one you take away and work on.

Instead of speaking in halting or incomplete sentences/thoughts like most people, you must learn to start speaking in complete sentences/thoughts. If you listen to anybody who has a commanding voice and presence and is an outstanding communicator, you will notice that they speak in COMPLETE sentences or thoughts. They go from complete sentence to complete sentence, or complete thought to complete thought.

People with a high status voice do not speak by breaking up their sentences/thoughts or pausing in the middle of sentences/thoughts while they think about what they're saying. By avoiding this behavior, they come off as completely sure of themselves and absolutely certain about what they are saying. If you speak in halting sentences/thoughts, you come off uncertain about what you are saying, and you will lack that "eloquence" that people find attractive.

So, the moral of the story is: You may only pause in places that are NATURAL for there to be a pause. Either at the end of a sentence, or at the end of a complete thought within a sentence. If you pause where it is not natural to pause, then you will come off as uncertain about what you are trying to express.

The way I have learned to do this is by starting to do my thinking BETWEEN sentences instead of pausing in the middle of a sentence to think about what I am saying. I will go from complete thought to complete thought without pausing anywhere in the middle of a thought. After a complete thought, I will pause if necessary to do my thinking, and then just start speaking another complete sentence/thought.

Do this instead of doing your thinking while you're in the middle of a thought. If you pause in the middle of a thought to think, you risk speaking in halting sentences or phrases and coming off as being unsure. It is these short pauses in the middle of sentences or thoughts that undermine your certainty and credibility.

Keep in mind you don't have to go crazy with this step. The occasional halting sentence is fine as we are all human, but try to eliminate halting sentences by at least 90%.

(Make sure you access the SPECIAL BONUS videos for examples of the ten steps at http:// www.artofverbalwar.com/vocalsuperstarbonus)

Chapter 6

Ten Steps to a High Status Voice

Step 2: Get Rid of Nasally or Throaty Sounds

In Step 2, you will get rid of any nasalness or throatiness in your voice. In other words, you are going to start speaking with a "diaphragm" voice, meaning your vocal tone will start to come from your diaphragm instead of your nose, throat, or chest.

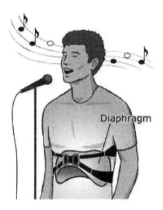

If you don't know where your diaphragm is, check out the above picture.

This step also addresses the CERTAINTY and AUTHORITY aspects of having a high-status voice. A nasal or throaty voice sounds constricted and therefore, a bit unsure and lacking power.

As I have mentioned before, having a CERTAIN voice isn't so much about the things you do to develop certainty, but more about getting rid of things that signal uncertainty.

I'm going to tell you why this step really matters: I used to have a paralegal that worked for me who was actually very competent and a pleasure to work with. However, he had this habit of getting nasally and speaking in halting sentences whenever he was unsure or uncertain about what he was saying. I could literally know exactly when he was unsure of what he was saying because his voice would give it away like a really bad poker tell. It's amazing how much the voice can tell us about someone or what they are saying when you start knowing what to look for. So, now you know that if you have nasalness or throatiness in your voice, you MUST get rid of it. How do you do that?

There are six steps to reducing nasally or throaty sounds:

1. Correct your posture: Proper posture is perhaps the most important thing about good speech, and can get rid of a nasal voice in a snap. Improper posture (stooping or slouching) will force you to speak through your nose. Here are some ways to correct your posture while you're speaking: Keep your back straight. You don't have to keep your back ramrod straight like you joined the Marines, but just keep a natural position and keep your ribcage open and relaxed so you have room for air.

2. Look straight ahead: A nasal voice can also be developed if you bow or tilt your head when speaking. When you speak, let your windpipe have as much room as possible to draw air to your diaphragm.

3. Relax your shoulders: When you lift up your shoulders, you end up constraining your windpipe. When you speak, let your shoulders fall into a natural position. Don't slouch, but keep your shoulders relaxed.

4. Breathe properly: All of the previous steps add up to allow you to breathe properly. After doing the first three steps, make sure you breathe properly by taking in just the right amount of air. If you take in too little air when you speak, you'll end up with a very exhausted, hushed tone that comes across as nasal. If you take in too much air, your nasal passages expand and more sound resonates through the space, giving you a nasal voice. People who don't speak from the diaphragm also don't breathe from the diaphragm. To breathe correctly, simply inhale and let your belly rise, and exhale and let your belly fall.

5. Finally, speak based on diaphragmatic breathing: Whether you're speaking, project from your diaphragm.

6. Double check yourself: Try making a nasal sound, then a throaty sound, then follow Steps 1 through 5 above and create a diaphragmatic sound. By doing this, it will become very apparent which voice sounds best.

(Make sure you access the SPECIAL BONUS videos for examples of the ten steps at http://www.artofverbalwar.com/vocalsuperstarbonus)

Chapter 7

Ten Steps to a High Status Voice

Step 3: Get Rid of Filler Words or Words Seeking Validation From Your Speech

This next step also addresses the CERTAINTY aspect of a high status voice. Using filler words as part of your speech make you come off as uncertain. Again, sounding certain is a matter of avoiding behaviors that make you come off as uncertain.

Here are the filler words you need to get rid of as being part of your speech:

"Um"
"Uh"
"Like"
"Ah"
"So"
"Hmm"
"Really"
"Cool"

In addition, it also will help your certainty by getting rid of other types of words which show you are looking for validation. You may not be actually looking for validation when you speak, but using these words will make your audience also feel as if you are uncertain, as if you are not quite sure about what you are saying and require their validation or approval about what you are saying.

"Right?"
"You know?"
"Got it?"

Be content with what you are saying and take complete ownership. After you make a statement, don't use any words seeking validation. Just be silent and let your words get absorbed and taken in by your audience.

Keep in mind you don't have to go crazy with this step. The occasional filler word is fine, but try to eliminate your usage of filler words by at least 90%.

(Make sure you access the SPECIAL BONUS videos for examples of the ten steps at http:// www.artofverbalwar.com/vocalsuperstarbonus)

Chapter 8

Ten Steps to a High Status Voice

Step 4: Eliminate Uncertain Tones From Speech

This next step also addresses CERTAINTY.

Have you ever met a person who makes any statement they say end up sounding like a question? I'm sure we all know quite a few people who do this unwittingly. In fact, we probably do it from time to time too. If you are sure you don't, you can skip this step and go on to Step 5.

The way people perform this status lowering behavior is by ending almost every sentence with an "uptone". NEVER end your sentences with an uptone. If you do that, you sound very uncertain about what you're saying. People who are not certain about what they are saying tend to do this, and its like a really bad poker tell. Its a tell that tells everybody that you don't know what you're talking about.

Remember: At the end of any statement, make sure you lower your intonation!

Having said this, uptones at the beginning of sentences are very useful, and you should learn how to incorporate them into your speech. I will talk about this further in Step 7.

(Make sure you access the SPECIAL BONUS videes for examples of the ten steps at http:// www.artofverbalwar.com/vocalsuperstarbonus)

SOURCE:

"When compared to confident statements, close-to-confident and unconfident expressions elicit-
ed reduced N1 and P2 responses and a late positivity from 900 to 1250 ms; unconfident and
close-to-confident expressions were differentiated later in the 1250-1600 ms time window."

-"Neural Responses Towards a Speaker's Feeling of (Un)knowing" (Jiang X, Pell MD 2016)

"These findings provide the first piece of evidence how quickly the brain responds to vocal cues
signifying the extent of a speaker's confidence during online speech comprehension; first, a
rough dissociation between unconfident and confident voices occurs as early as 200 ms after
speech onset."

-On How the Brian Decodes Vocal Cues About Speaker Confidence (Jiang X, Pell MD 2015)

Chapter 9

Ten Steps to a High Status Voice

Step 5: Project Your Voice

This step addresses the CERTAINTY and AUTHORITY aspects of a high status voice.

In my old corporate job, I started work on the same day as another lady. I was joining the company to be the in-house legal counsel. She was joining to become head of a marketing group. The marketing group was a one-person team, meaning she was the only person on the team. Fast forward just a few years and she became Chief Operating Officer of the firm.

I remember her distinctly when I met her on that first day. She had a distinct and strong high volume voice. It was loud and bossy sounding. Well, it was so bossy, she became my boss and everyone else's boss! If you listen to her speak, her voice is distinctly high status. With a high status voice comes higher work status.

So the moral of the story is: When you speak, you need to be louder than you think. Don't yell, but instead of speaking at people, speak THROUGH people. Having a louder voice means you are CONFIDENT and CERTAIN in what you say.

(Make sure you access the SPECIAL BONUS videos for examples of the ten steps at http:// www.artofverbalwar.com/vocalsuperstarbonus)

Chapter 10

Ten Steps to a High Status Voice

Step 6: Bring Emotion and Energy to Your Voice

Now that we have gone over five steps that address CERTAINTY, this step addresses the CAP-TIVATING aspect of a high status voice. The reason why most of us are not captivating when we speak and we end up speaking in a flat, two dimensional way is because we are not speaking with an emotion in mind while we speak.

Actors are taught to choose an emotion that they are trying to portray in their acting. Once they are clear on the emotion they want to portray, they are taught to recall a time when they feel that emotion using all five senses and incorporate that emotion into their acting. This is exactly what you should be doing when you are speaking if you want to be captivating.

So before you have an important conversation or presentation, you need to focus emotionally. This is even true when you are making a phone call. Phone lines are known to remove emotion from speech, so some people are even taught to smile when they are talking on the phone even though the other person cannot see them. By doing that, they bring appropriate emotion to the call.

In addition to emotion, you also need to bring energy to your voice. There is no magic pill here. You just need to make sure that your voice projects energy at all times. If your speech lacks energy, it will fail to captivate.

(Make sure you access the SPECIAL BONUS videos for examples of the ten steps at http://www.artofverbalwar.com/vocalsuperstarbonus)

SOURCE:

"Emotional prosody reduces hemispheric asymmetry for linguistic processing: Findings are consistent with the hypothesis that the right hemisphere is better able to process speech when it carries emotional prosody."

-"Emotional Language is All Right" (Godfrey HK, Grimshaw GM 2015)

"Recognition performance was comparable for words studied with emotional and neutral prosody. However, subsequent valence ratings indicted that study prosody changed the affective representation of words in memory. Compared to words with neutral prosody, words with sad prosody were later rated as more negative and words with happy prosody were later rated as more positive."

-Mark My Words: Tone of Voice Changes Affective Word Representations in Memory" (A Schemer 2010)

Chapter 11

Ten Steps to a High Status Voice

Step 7: Incorporate Variety in Your Speaking Patterns

This step also goes towards the CAPTIVATING aspect of a high status voice.

I know I said in Step 5 that you need to learn to speak louder. However, this is NOT always the case. Sometimes, if you want someone to really pay attention, you can shout, but if you want them to really hear you and believe you, whisper it as if its a secret. People don't always believe others who are loud. Sometimes in order to be captivating, you actually want to deliver something in HUSHED tones. This is what "variety" in speaking patterns means.

When speaking, you want to give a performance that has variety. There are different ways you can vary your speaking patterns:

- Pitch (high/low)
- Volume (loud/soft)
- Tone (resonant, hollow)
- Tempo (fast, slow)
- Rhythm (fluid, staccato)
- Placement of pauses (end of sentences/end of thoughts/concepts)
- Placement of uptones (anywhere except the end of a statement)
- How quickly you start a sentence after finishing a sentence.

From sentence to sentence, play with these different aspects to EMPHASIZE important things. Play with them also to just give a varied and interesting performance. Say goodbye to flat conversations, and start being captivating.

A special note on uptones: I know I said uptones are bad. They are terrible at the end of statements. I know you will never break that rule, promise me that. However, uptones at the beginning of sentences can be very good to add variety to your vocal delivery. An uptone at the beginning of a sentence will signal to a listener that its time to pay attention. Don't overuse them, but they can add excellent variety to your performance.

Somebody I like listening to is Colin Cowherd, the sports commentator who works for Fox Sports as of the date of this book. He's known to say incorrect and illogical things, but his voice is so high status, i.e. captivating, authoritative, and certain, sometimes its hard not to believe the things he says. Listen to his morning show or podcast to get a feel for someone who has incredible command of his voice and always gives a perfectly varied vocal performance. He's never boring when he speaks!

(Make sure you access the SPECIAL BONUS videos for examples of the ten steps at http://www.artofverbalwar.com/vocalsuperstarbonus)

SOURCE:

"Through applying multivariate logistic regression we found that initial pitch that significantly deviated from the speaker's median pitch level was predictive of the social action of the question...this latter finding reveals a kind of iconicity in the relationship between prosody and social action in which a marked pitch correlates with a marked social action. Thus, we argue that speakers rely on pitch to provide an early signal for recipients that the question is not to be interpreted through its literal semantics but rather through an inference."

-"Marked Initial Pitch in Questions Signals Marked Communicative Function" (Sicoli MA, Sitvers T, Enfield NJ, Gevinson SC 2015)

Chapter 12

Ten Steps to a High Status Voice

Step 8: Maintain the Natural Rhythm of Phrases

This step goes towards the CERTAINTY aspect of a high status voice. While in Step 7 I urged you to incorporate variety into your vocal delivery, do not change up the natural rhythm of phrases.

Every phrase in the English language has a natural rhythm; in other words, there is a way that each phrase SHOULD sound and be phrased. Using Step 1 and this Step 7, you need to ensure that you are not breaking up phrases that need to naturally sound a specific way. If you break up a phrase's natural phrasing, you will sound uncertain about what you are saying.

In addition to natural phrasing, you also need to make sure you are emphasizing the right words in a phrase. For a given meaning, there is a natural place where the phrase must be emphasized. If you fail to make emphasis where you should be making emphasis, your delivery will sound flat, so play close attention to these two things: natural phrasing and correct emphasis of important words.

(Make sure you access the SPECIAL BONUS videos for examples of the ten steps at http:// www.artofverbalwar.com/vocalsuperstarbonus)

Chapter 13

Ten Steps to a High Status Voice

Step 9: Find Your Most Ideal and Pleasing Resonance/Pitch

This step addresses the CAPTIVATING aspect of a high status voice.

Step 9 is about developing a pleasing resonance and pitch for your specific voice. Everyone's voice and body (especially the vocal cords) has certain constraints, so everybody has an different ideal pitch for his/her voice. We just want to find that ideal pitch for your body and vocal cords in this step.

The ideal pitch for your voice produces a pleasing resonance for your voice, which creates the CAPTIVATING aspect of your voice. "Resonance" means a strong and pleasing tone. I won't say "deep" because that is not necessarily the aim. Some people have a natural pitch that is not necessarily deep, but because they are speaking at their ideal pitch, the tone is pleasing. Keep in mind that deeper isn't better if it sounds forced and unnatural.

It is said that the most attractive voice is not the voice which is deeper, but the voice that is phonating most freely and naturally. Finding the most pleasing resonance for your voice is about finding the right vocal pitch for your voice. The right vocal pitch helps you be a more effective communicator. It is at this pitch or roughly around this pitch that we will call your "home base". Keep in mind, you can go higher or lower than your home base to provide vocal variety, but only temporarily. You are going to spend most of your time at the home base pitch or roughly around it.

Here are the steps for finding your ideal pitch and resonance:

1. First, breathe (i) through your nose (ii) into your belly (see Step 2 again if you are having trouble with this).

2. Then, feel a yawn in the back of your throat. This should push your oropharynx back, elongating the middle of your vocal tract.

3. Finally, say "uh-huh" as if you were casually saying "yes" to a friend's question. The ideal pitch of your voice when you speak should match the pitch of the "uh" that you create.

There you go, now you have found your ideal pitch. Play around with it and see how you sound when speaking now. Better huh?

(Make sure you access the SPECIAL BONUS videos for examples of the ten steps at http://www.artofverbalwar.com/vocalsuperstarbonus)

SOURCE:

"Results from congenital amuse: Results from these experiments suggest an influence of low frequency information in identifying emotional content of speech."

-"Sound Frequency Affects Speech Emotion Perception" (Lolli SL 2015)

Chapter 14

Ten Steps to a High Status Voice

Step 10: Maintain Your Vocal Tonality In Pressure Situations

This final step goes towards the AUTHORITY aspect of a high status voice. The interesting thing is this "step" isn't necessarily something you DO to develop an authoritative voice. It's more like a final exam.

The true test of a high status voice is someone who can keep his/her high status vocal tonality in situations that are uncomfortable. There is no greater test. If you are truly high status, and your voice is truly high status, then when you are faced with a stressful situation or other people with status around you, your voice should not change.

Back to my former paralegal that I spoke about in Step 2: Remember his voice would give off all sorts of tells when I would question him about certain things and he felt uncertain? His voice would tremble slightly, his pitch would change, his voice would get nasally, and he would speak in halting sentences. Obviously, this reflected the fact that I was his supervisor and he was my direct report. He felt uncomfortable being questioned and that manifested itself in changes to his voice tonality while speaking to me.

When I was a teenager and completely unconfident with and around girls, every time I talked to a girl, my voice would change from its natural pitch and tone to a higher pitch and softer tone. I can't believe I'm admitting this, but its true. Needless to say, I was no ladies man in high school. Again, these situations would manifest itself in changes to my voice.

The moral of the story is, the voice is a window to your status and authority. It can betray you (and your status) to other people much quicker than your words can. Listeners can detect and perceive even the slightest variation in vocal cues.

In a Kent State University study (cited below), researchers found that when two people talk, the person who changes their normal, vocal characteristics the LEAST will be perceived to have higher status than the other person. The person who changes his/her vocal tonality to match the other person's becomes the lower status person in that relationship.

So, NEVER change your vocal tonality when communicating with other people. You need to be vigilant about this and always monitor yourself when speaking with others, and you need to practice this step deliberately over time. Make other people's vocal tonality mirror yours. DON'T let your voice tremble, and don't change your natural vocal volume (which should naturally err on the side of being louder than softer) just because other people with high status enter the room or just because you are in a high pressure situation. A high status person doesn't let external events change who they are; if you are truly high status, you will let your true and natural voice shine through in any situation.

(Make sure you access the SPECIAL BONUS videes for examples of the ten steps at http:// www.artofverbalwar.com/vocalsuperstarbonus**)**

SOURCE:

"Correlation coefficients from comparisons of partners' voice spectra and factor analysis of the correlation matrix showed that lower status partners accommodated their voices to higher status partners via the nonverbal signal. Student ratings of the social status of the same talk show host and guests were correlated with factor loadings, thereby providing convergent validity of the nonverbal signal as a predictor of social status perceptions and accommodation."

-"A Nonverbal Signal in Voices of Interview Partners Effectively Predicts Accommodation and Social Status Perceptions" (Gregory S 1996)

Chapter 15

Ten Steps to a High Status Voice

Step 11: Don't Drag Vowel Sounds

This bonus step goes towards the CERTAINTY aspect of a high status voice and is related to Step 1.

In Step 1, I talked about how you should not pause in any place where it is not natural to pause. In addition to eliminating unnatural pauses, you also need to eliminate any dragging vowel sounds. Dragging vowel sounds are similar to pauses because you end up sounding like you are stuck for words. Whether you are stuck for words or not, dragging any vowels within a word makes you sound UNCERTAIN about what you are saying.

(Make sure you access the SPECIAL BONUS videos for examples of the ten steps at http:// www.artofverbalwar.com/vocalsuperstarbonus)

Chapter 16

Conclusion and Next Steps

Here we are at the end of Vocal Superstar! After reading about the ten steps to a high status voice, I hope it has become clear what you need to work on to develop your high status voice. You may already have some of the steps firmly in place, so just work on the steps that you do not yet have down.

I can't wait to hear about the results you get in life after fully implementing this program. I hope it will profoundly alter your life in a positive way. Keep in mind that this is NOT going to be an overnight transformation. It's more of a 3 to 6 month transformation if you work on improving your voice delivery deliberately.

Here are some suggestions for how you can take this material forward on your own and make significant progress over the next 3 to 6 months:

1. Find and model great speakers with high status voices. You want to practice speaking like them. Just talk along while you listen to them. Emulate the things they do with their voice and presentation. By doing that, you will absorb their vocal patterns and delivery.

2. Videotape or record yourself once a week and track your progress. Just speak for 1-2 minutes into a recorder and check how you sound. Don't do this with a script, you want to do this off the top of your head. There is no truer test than recording yourself and it will be very evident what you need to work on week to week.

3. Continue to work on diaphragmatic breathing. If you are not a diaphragmatic breather, this is changing a well ingrained habit, and so you will need to work on this very deliberately.

Thanks for checking out Vocal Superstar!

Here's to your new superstar voice,
Min Liu

SPECIAL BONUS ANNOUNCEMENT

As a gift for reading this entire book, I have a SPECIAL BONUS for you! Go to www.artofverbalwar.com/vocalsuperstarbonus and you will receive a secret link to videos illustrating each of the ten steps laid out in this book.

NEXT STEPS

1. **ACCESS** your special bonus at www.artofverbalwar.com/vocalsuperstarbonus

2. Leave a positive **REVIEW** of this book on Amazon so that others can benefit from it at http://amzn.to/1TQBBuS

3. **SUBSCRIBE** to my Youtube channel and learn even more about other verbal skills at www.youtube.com/artofverbalwar

4. **CONTACT** me at info@artofverbalwar.com

5. **SHARE** this book with others.

THANK YOU FOR YOUR SUPPORT!

ABOUT THE AUTHOR

Min Liu is a corporate lawyer, Amazon #1 bestselling author, and the founder of The Art of Verbal War, where people learn to EXCEL in verbal skills.

Based in San Francisco, CA, Min's burning ambition is to teach like-minded people how to give their gifts and value to the world by helping them become EXCEPTIONAL in verbal skills, persuasion, influence and power.

In the words of his readers, he's the "older brother you've never had", and as a real-life big brother himself, his mission is to show you the ropes in all the things school never taught you.

He's especially aroused by basketball, meditation, reading books on psychology and inspirational people, people who are value givers, and most of all, constantly breaking out of his comfort zone and helping others break out of theirs. On the other hand, he despises value suckers, mediocre mindsets, and most of all, wearing sweaters.

Media, speaking, one-to-one coaching requests, or other inquiries can be sent to info@artofverbalwar.com.

****

BOOKS BY MIN LIU

THE KING'S MINDSET: TWENTY MINDSETS TO TRANSFORM ORDINARY MEN INTO KINGS
The "roadmap" to extraordinary success in life

THE NEW ART OF BEING RIGHT: 38 WAYS TO WIN AN ARGUMENT IN TO-DAY'S WORLD
A modernized version of Arthur Schopenhauer's "Art of Being Right", a playbook of strategies and tactics to help you win arguments in today's complicated society

VERBAL SELF DEFENSE 101
An introduction to verbal self defense

PEOPLE GAMES: THE TEN MOST COMMON POWER PLAYS AND MIND GAMES THAT PEOPLE PLAY
Learn how to defend yourself from mind games and power plays

PEOPLE GAMES AT WORK: POWER PLAYS, MIND GAMES & WORKPLACE BULLYING
Learn how to rid yourself of workplace bullies

To learn more about my books:
www.artofverbalwar.com/books

****

****

COURSES BY MIN LIU

VERBAL SELF DEFENSE FOR THE SOCIALLY INTELLIGENT
A system for defending yourself from verbal bullying, attacks, and insults with wit and social intelligence

VERBAL DOMINATION
An online course about dominating and winning verbal confrontations

THE HARVEY SPECTER GUIDE
An online course about how to win big, inspired by the character Harvey Specter of the TV show "Suits"

AND MORE...

To learn more about my courses:
www.artofverbalwar.com/courses

****

29703043R10021

Printed in Great Britain
by Amazon